THE
MONTEREY
PENINSULA
AND
SCENIC HIGHWAY 1

D1415482

Design & Layout: Ken Glaser, Jr.

Monterey Marina Aerial

Aerial of Monterey

Fisherman's Wharf

MONTEREY BAY SEALIFE

Monterey Bay is abundant with sealife of all types and species. From the playful sea otters and harbor seals, to the loud barking sea lions and majestic migrating whales heading south for the winter, Monterey Bay is spectacular at all times of the year.

Fisherman's Wharf and Cannery Row are two of the most popular destinations on the Monterey Peninsula. The Wharf is famous for its great restaurants and shops and the fresh crab and calamari served at the open seafood stands. Cannery Row, made famous by John Steinbeck in his many novels, is home to the world famous Monterey Bay Aquarium and many fine restaurants, stores and hotels.

ROW

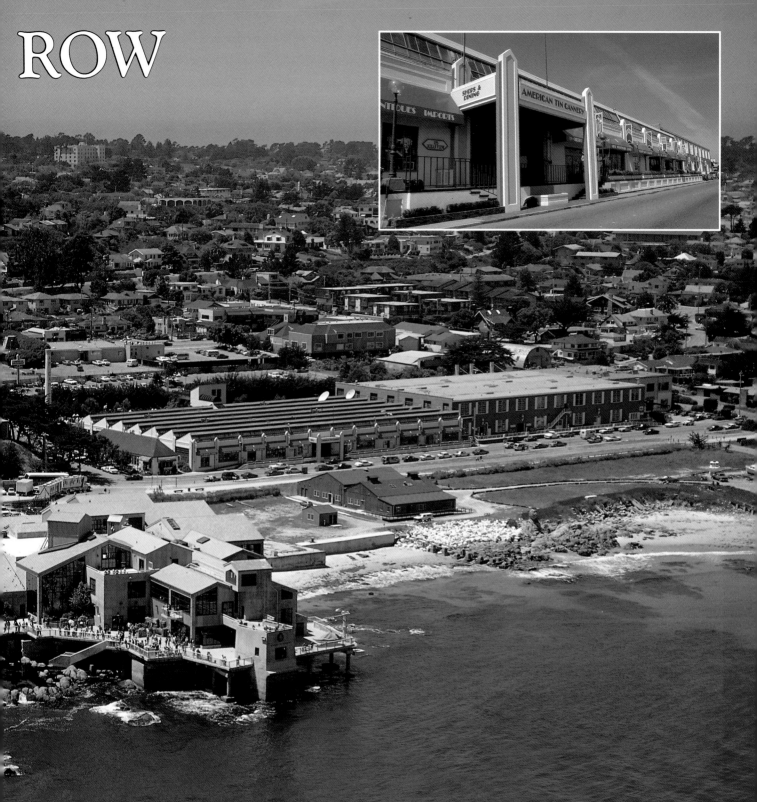

MONTEREY BAY AQUARIUM-This amazing array of exhibits
ranks among the world's finest. The Aquarium is located
on Cannery Row and features the habitats of Monterey Bay.

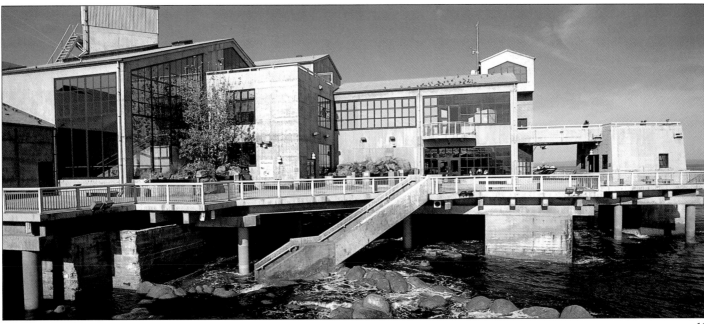

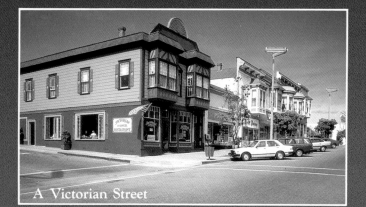

A Victorian Street

GROVE

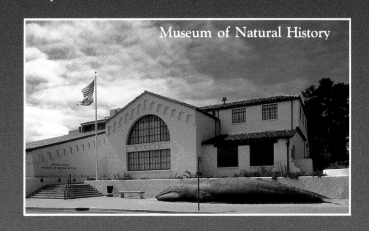

Museum of Natural History

PACIFIC GROVE-A lovely shoreline, covered by the lustrous red and pink "Ice Plant", fronts a city of well-maintained Victorian homes and superb restaurants.

Pacific Grove, with its lustrous blanket of pink Ice Plant as seen from the air.
Laguna-Seca Raceway brings "Indy" cars to the Monterey Peninsula.

Pacific Grove is world famous for the annual migration of the Monarch Butterflies. During the migration season, the sky is full of fluttering wings of this beautiful species.

Seventeen-Mile Drive, renowned throughout the world,
may be entered at several points; Pacific Grove Gate,
Carmel Gate, Highway 1 Gate, and Country Club Gate.

VIEW FROM CYPRESS POINT LOOKOUT

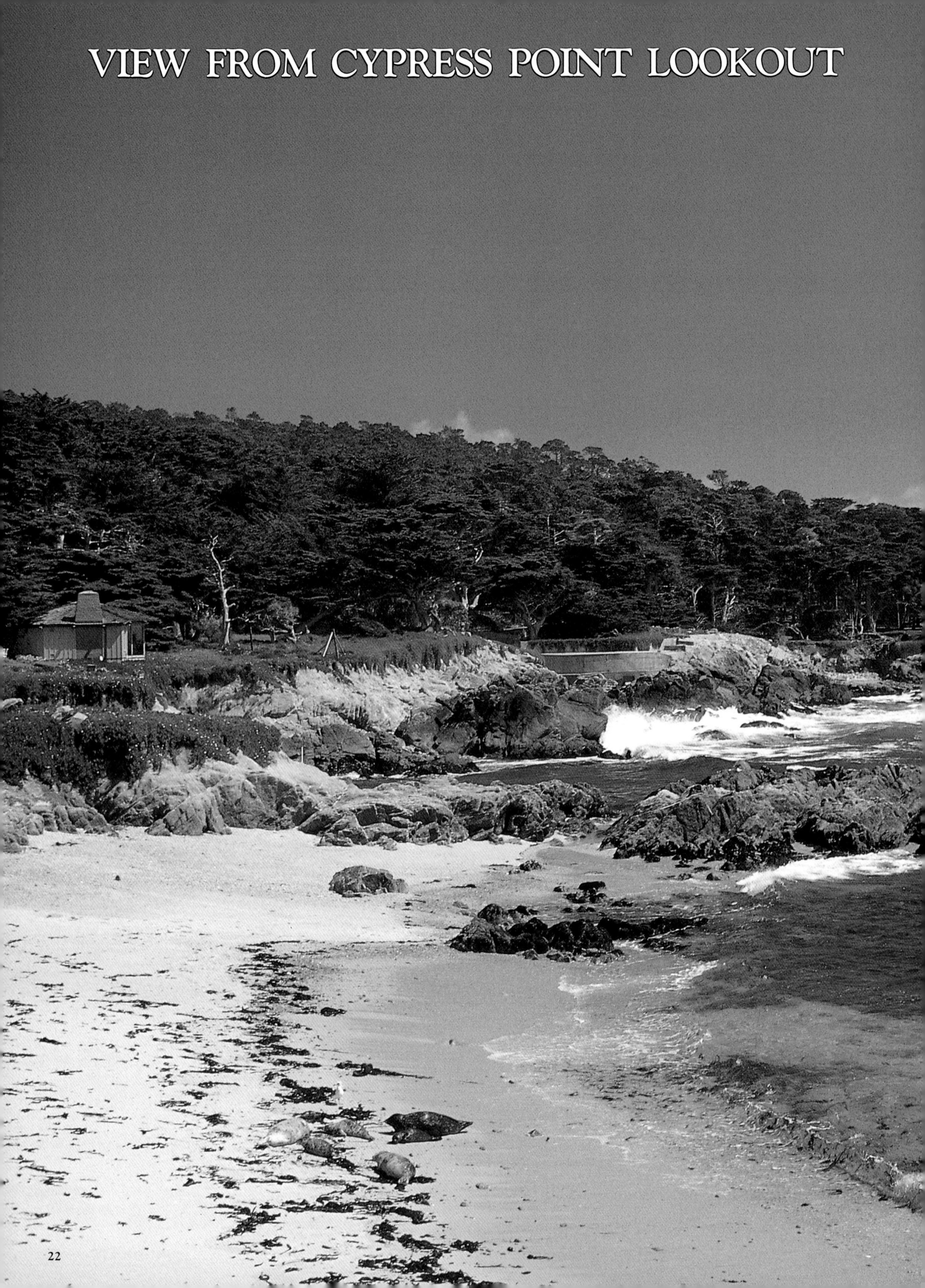

FRIENDLY DEER ON 17 MILE DRIVE

LONE CYPRESS

The Lone Cypress-Clinging to what is nearly bare
rock, this lone tree keeps its vigil.
It is considered to be the world's most photgraphed tree.

A Timeless Cypress

Cypress Point Golf Course-A private club with a world-wide reputation. This superior
layout includes some of golf's most beautiful holes, by the crashing surf of Monterey Bay.

PEBBLE BEACH LODGE AND GOLF LINKS-A world-class resort and one of the top ten ranked golf courses in a magnificent setting on Carmel Bay. The course was the site of the 1972 and 1982 U.S. Open Tournaments as well as the 1977 PGA. It is instantly recognizable as the former home of the "Bing Crosby" Pro-Am Tournament, now known as the AT & T Pebble Beach National Pro-Am.

The "Bing Crosby" Hall of Fame

A Cypress on Carmel Beach

Home at Carmel

39

CARMEL - This quaint and unique town is known for the galleries and workshops of its world famous artist colony. Located on Carmel Bay, the town has wonderful restaurants, great shopping, cozy inn's with fireplaces, and beautiful homes and cottages set among the pine trees and along the rocky coast. Carmel's beautiful beach, at the foot of Ocean Avenue, is in walking distance from any part of the town, and is a must visit at sunset.

Carmel is and was home to many famous poets, artists and photographers. Below is pictured the home of Robinson Jefers, a famous poet. Other famous residents who at one time resided in this town are Ansel Adams, Imogene Cunningham, Merv Griffin, Doug McClure, Paul Anka and the former mayor, Clint Eastwood.

Mission San Carlos Borromeo-This famous Mission, faithfully maintained, was established by Father Junipero Serra in 1770. It is one of the oldest missions in California. Father Serra's remains are interred at the foot of the high altar. The Mission is open to the public and visitors are welcome.

THE BARNYARD - A quaint collection of shops, restaurants and services in keeping with the nature of Carmel.

Carmel Valley

PT. LOBOS STATE RESERVE-South of Carmel is this ruggedly beautiful headland maintained as a California State Reserve. Its name is derived from the barking sounds of the sea lion colonies on its offshore rocks which carries inland as the howling of seawolves.

China Cove

The rugged coastline at Point Lobos

California's coastline south of Carmel

The Big Sur Lighthouse stands a lonely vigil guiding mariners safely away from danger.

HEARST CASTLE

This magnificent complex, which
defies adequate description, was
created on a dominant overlook
of the Pacific Ocean. It was
envisioned and commissioned by
William Randolph Hearst, a publishing
giant and heir to a massive fortune
amassed by his father, a gold mining
genius.